Symbols of Freedom

National Parks

Big Bend National Park

M.C. Hall

Heinemann Library
Chicago, Illinois

Customer Service 888-454-2279
Visit our website at www.heinemannlibrary.com

Page layout by Richard Parker and Maverick Design
Photo research by Maria Joannou
Illustrations by Jeff Edwards
Printed and bound in China by South China Printing Company Limited

10 09 08 07 06
10 9 8 7 6 5 4 3 2 1

Library of Congress Cataloging-in-Publication Data
Hall, Margaret, 1947-
    Big Bend National Park / Margaret Hall.
        p. cm. -- (National parks)
Includes bibliographical references (p.   ) and index.
ISBN 1-4034-6697-1 (lib. bdg. : alk. paper) -- ISBN 1-4034-6704-8 (pbk. : alk. paper)
1. Big Bend National Park (Tex.)--Juvenile literature. I. Title.
    F392.B53H35 2005
    976.4'932--dc22

                        2004030473

Acknowledgments
The author and publishers are grateful to the following for permission to reproduce copyright material:
Alamy pp. **17**, **26**; Bill Pogue p. **5**; Corbis p. **15** (Buddy Mays), p. **11** (Chris Rainier), pp. **9**, **12**, **16**, **18**, (David Muench), pp. **4**, **23**, (Tom Bean); Brand X pp. **29**, **30**, **31**, **32**; FLPA p. **19** (Tim Fitzharris/ Minden Pictures), p. **7** (Wil Meinderts/ Foto Natura); Getty Images/Photodisc p. **14**; Library of Congress p. **8**; National Park Service p. **24** a, p. **24** inset; Naturepl p. **21** (Tom Vezo); NHPA p. **22** (Stephen Krasemann), NHPA p. **20** (T Kitchin & V Hurst); Photographers Direct p. **10**; Photolibrary.com/ Oxford Scientific Films p. **13** (Clay Willard); Science Photo Library (NOAO / AURA /NSF) p. **25**; Topham Picturepoint p. **27** (Bob Daemmrich/ The Image Works)

Cover photograph of Big Bend National Park reproduced with permission of PhotoLibrary.com (Robin Bush)

Every effort has been made to contact copyright holders of any material reproduced in this book.
Any omissions will be rectified in subsequent printings if notice is given to the publisher.

Some words are shown in bold, **like this**. You can find out what they mean by looking in the glossary.

Contents

Our National Parks

National parks are areas set aside for people to visit and enjoy **nature**. The land in national parks is protected. People cannot cut down trees or pick plants in a national park.

National Parks belong to all the people.

BIG BEND
NATIONAL PARK

PAY ENTRANCE FEE
PANTHER JUNCTION
VISITOR CENTER
20 MILES

There are more than 50 national parks in the United States. Big Bend National Park is one of the country's most interesting parks.

Big Bend National Park is located in the southwestern part of Texas. The Rio Grande flows along the southern edge of the park.

This river makes a big bend near the park. That is where Big Bend gets its name. The country of **Mexico** is on the other side of the river.

the Rio Grande

Big Bend Long Ago

For thousands of years, Native Americans traveled through the Big Bend area on hunting trips. Later, the Chisos **tribe** lived near Big Bend. After that, **ranchers** raised **cattle** on the land.

People thought Big Bend was an interesting and unusual place. They wanted to save it for others to enjoy. In 1933 Big Bend became a **state park**. In 1944 it became a **national park**.

Summers are very hot at Big Bend National Park. Most visitors come in March and April, when the weather is cooler.

There are many things to do at the park. Visitors can camp, hike, and look at **wildlife**. They can also fish and boat in the Rio Grande.

The Chihuahuan Desert

The Chihuahuan **Desert** covers most of Big Bend National Park. Cactuses and other plants that do not need much water grow there.

century plant

Sometimes it rains in the desert. Then visitors can see many beautiful wildflowers. The flowers only bloom for a few days.

The Rio Grande

The Rio Grande is an important part of Big Bend National Park. In some places the river is very wide. It flows through grassy fields.

Other parts of the river go through deep canyons. The water flows very fast there. People enjoy riding **rafts** through the fast-moving water.

The Mountains

Most visitors spend time in the mountains of the park. Some small trees grow on the mountain slopes. It is cooler there than in the **desert**.

People camp and hike in the mountains. In some places, the mountains form sharp peaks. The trails are steep and rocky.

Rocky Places

the chimneys

Big Bend is very rocky. The wind blows sand and dirt against the rocks. After thousands of years the rocks have been worn down into interesting shapes.

There are trails that go through fields of huge **boulders**. Some rocks balance on top of each other. There are even rocks that make a window visitors can look through!

The Animals of Big Bend

Many snakes, toads, and lizards live in the **desert**. The spadefoot toad stays underground until there is rain. Deer, mountain lions, and black bears live in the mountains, where the weather is cooler.

mountain lion

Fish and turtles live in the park's river and ponds. Big Bend is the only place in the world where the mosquitofish is found. It only lives in one small pond in the park!

red-eared turtle

Many kinds of bats live in caves and trees in Big Bend. Visitors see the bats when it starts to get dark. That is when the bats leave their nests.

Big Bend is also a favorite place for **birdwatchers**. Birds like the Peregrine falcon are **endangered**. The elf owl is a bird that only lives in the southwest of the United States and **Mexico**.

cactus wren

People sometimes find dinosaur bones at Big Bend. In 1999 a scientist found bones of a huge dinosaur called Alamosaurus!

The Alamosaurus bones were moved to a museum.

Visitors also come to Big Bend National Park to see the stars. There are no cities or towns nearby. The night sky is so dark that the stars are easy to see.

Park Buildings and People

There are four visitor centers in Big Bend National Park. People visit the centers to learn about the park. Some centers have campgrounds nearby where visitors can stay.

Panther Junction Visitor Center

Park rangers teach visitors about the plants and animals in the park. They also take people on hikes. Children who visit Big Bend can become Junior Rangers.

Map of Big Bend National Park

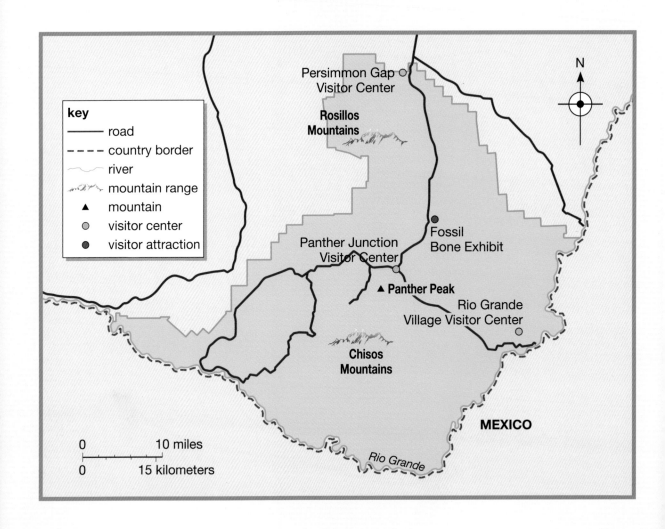

key
— road
- - - country border
〜 river
⌃⌃⌃ mountain range
▲ mountain
◯ visitor center
● visitor attraction

Persimmon Gap ◯
Visitor Center

Rosillos Mountains

N

● Fossil
Bone Exhibit

Panther Junction
Visitor Center ◯

▲ **Panther Peak**

Rio Grande
Village Visitor Center ◯

Chisos Mountains

MEXICO

Rio Grande

0   10 miles

0   15 kilometers

Timeline

10,000 years ago	Native tribes hunt in the Big Bend area
1500s–1800s	Chisos **tribe** settles in the Big Bend area
Early 1700s	Apache tribes' war chases the Chisos from the area
1800s	Mexican settlers move into the Big Bend region to raise **cattle**
1845	Texas becomes part of the United States
Early 1900s	Miners dig for **cinnabar** in Big Bend
1933	Part of Big Bend becomes a Texas **state park**
1944	Big Bend becomes a **national park**
1946	Cabins and a store are built in the park
1999	Dinosaur bones are found in the park

Glossary

birdwatcher person who watches birds and keeps track of what he or she sees

boulder large rock

cattle cows raised for meat or milk

cinnabar red rock that contains a metal once used for making bombs

desert place that does not get much rain

endangered in danger of becoming extinct, or dying out

Mexico country that is south of the United States

national park natural area set aside by the government for people to visit

nature the outdoors and the wild plants and animals found there

park ranger man or woman who works in a national park and shares information about the wildlife and unusual sights of the park

raft floating platform used for moving things over water

rancher person who raises animals on a large area of land called a ranch

state park natural area set aside by a state for people to visit

tribe Native American group

wildlife wild animals of an area

Find Out More

Books

An older reader can help you with these books:

Gaines, Richard. *The Comanche*. Mankato, Minn.: Checkerboard Books, 2000.

Galko, Francine. *Desert Animals*. Chicago, Ill.: Heinemann Library, 2003.

Marsh, Carole. *My First Book About Texas*. Peachtree City, Ga.: Gallopade International, 2002.

O'Mara, Anna. *Deserts*. Mankato, Minn.: Bridgestone Books, 1999.

Parker, Laurie. *Texas Alphabet*. Brandon, Miss.: Quail Ridge Press, 2000.

Zappler, George. *Learn About Texas Dinosaurs*. Austin, Tex.: Texas Parks and Wildlife Press, 2001.

Address

To find out more about Big Bend National Park, write to:

Big Bend National Park
P.O. Box 129
Big Bend National Park, TX 79834

Index